ONLY BLUE BODY

ANHINGA PRESS

Only Blue Body

Rosalynde Vas Dias

2011 Robert Dana-Anhinga
Prize for Poetry

Selected by Terese Svoboda

ANHINGA PRESS
TALLAHASSEE, FLORIDA 2012

Cover art: "Horse with Pretty Hair," by Xander Marro
Author photograph: Robert Houllahan
Cover and text design: Carol Lynne Knight
Type Styles: titles and text set in Adobe Garamond Pro

Library of Congress Cataloging-in-Publication Data
Only Blue Body by Rosalynde Vas Dias, First Edition
ISBN – 978-1-934695-29-6
Library of Congress Cataloging Card Number – 2012944955

Anhinga Press Inc. is a non-profit corporation
dedicated wholly to the publication and appreciation
of fine poetry and other literary genres.

For personal orders, catalogs
and information write to:
Anhinga Press
P.O. Box 3665
Tallahassee, Florida 32315
Website: www.anhinga.org
Email: info@anhinga.org

Published in the United States
by Anhinga Press
Tallahassee, Florida
First Edition, 2012

Contents

ACKNOWLEDGMENTS

A version of "Moth Man" appeared in *Redivider*. "Pupil Dilated" was published in the Yarroway Mountain Press anthology, *Cadence of Hooves: A Celebration of Horses*. "Mosquito" was published in *The Cincinnati Review*. "Silent Defense" was published in *Crazyhorse*. The poems "Intruding Memory" and "Mechanized" appeared in the *Marsh Hawk Review*. "Equinox" and "Picture Book" appeared in *The Pinch*. "Otter at a Party" appeared in *Matter*. "Only Blue Body" is forthcoming in *West Branch*. "Hidden," "Model," and "Reoccurring" are all forthcoming in the *Laurel Review*. "No Wonder" is forthcoming in *The West Guide to Writing: Success from Community College to University* (Kendall Hunt Publishers, 2012).

First and foremost, thank you to my parents, Richard and Bernadette Vas Dias. You made me a reader and never discouraged me from trying to be a poet.

Thank you to my four wise and patient Warren Wilson advisors, Dana Levin, Van Jordan, Karen Brennan, and James Longenbach. Many of these poems were drafted and revised under their instruction. Thank you especially to Jim for prodding me along as I assembled the very first version of *Only Blue Body* during my thesis semester.

Thank you to poets Rick Bursky and David Ruekberg for your unflagging moral support and well-timed phone calls. Ross White, thank you so much for inviting me into the Grind Daily Writing series in 2007. That accidental invite gave me the poems needed to bring *Only Blue Body* to book-length as well as an extended writing family. Thank you generally, Ross, for your wonderful hyper-enthusiasm and overall awesomeness. You're a real role model.

Thank you also to Debra Gitterman who challenged me, in the wintery-spring of 2008, to bring *Only Blue Body* to book-length and to start submitting it.

Thanks to Kate Shapira, Providence poet and tireless poetry advocate, for reading *Only Blue Body* this year and for all the great stuff you do for poets and future poets.

Thank you, Terese Svoboda for selecting *Only Blue Body* for the Robert Dana Award and thank you, Rick Campbell and Lynne Knight of Anhinga Press, for guiding me through the exciting/scary publication process.

ONLY BLUE BODY

~

Only Blue Body

He wasn't speaking for all of us, the man
     in the lecture hall, saying very casually:

    The color

        of an anchor

    doesn't matter.

He wasn't speaking my thoughts.

      ~

    The peach-throated love bird,
pressed to the wall of the cage, head turned away.

    The mate shielding it.
Shielding with its own body. Prisoners

    who are lovers in a cage. An anchor
for the other. They are tender

    to me. *Peach-throated* — the green
halves of a single heart.

      ~

    Where am I?

I couldn't speak. My throat. Constricted
     point of light:

blue knot.

~

A photograph — a girl's body tied in rope, she has

blue skin.

I've always wanted dark

blue skin.

~

Back in the body

by accident.

Can't get back in

by trying.

~

But if the body were blue.
If I could tie myself

to the body as the body is tied
in the photograph —

shoulders straining back,
jaw tipped upward so the throat

is unguarded; if it were dark blue —
the only blue body in the world —

I could always find it.
It would always be mine.

Pupil Dilated

The horse is black.
Like a grackle: bronze-
green flash
when the neck
bends its long face toward me.

Or the horse is a grackle:
yellow-eyed,
short hops forward.
It flies up
like a horse's neck stretching

as it would stretch toward me,
so the muzzle may lip
oats from a flattened palm.
The bird in flight
keeps stretching

upward, hooves cutting
air or running over water,
skidding — there's an oil
skim — purple-green weeps
out and it's down,

down and sliding, as on slick
pavement, and the hide —
the horse's beautiful hide —
it's torn, torn down to red mash,
down to bone and yellow eye.

The air bends down
under the wing.
The air beats down. The wing
beats the air down.
Look down.

Don't look at the bird.
Don't see a horse.

HIDDEN

I used to be a doe goat
pirate, Captain of my own
ship in a picture book where the water-
color was deep and limpid and teaming.
I was a Toggenburg with a striped face
and udders hidden by my pirate
breeches. My crew was various —
a badger, a jaguar, some monkeys,
a crane. We got along because
it was fiction. Also, there seemed
little choice: we risked hanging
every day. The sea was wide and
storms wanted to swallow the ship
and erase us right out of the jewel-
colored pages of the world. Now,
I am merely a woman with breasts
on my chest and no crew whatsoever.
Animals don't talk to me anymore.
Not in a language I understand.
The ship is gone. Sailing on
without me? Or broken,
inert in that desert under the dark water?

PRINT

In snowy woods. Walking
through the black
trees. His back
to me. Snow gathering
in his hat brim.
A black hat in black
woods on white snow.
His back to me.

Wood Cut

At work across the room, he was silence —
        a book closed upon itself,
but like her

made of lines that curved: the curve of his body
        over his work,
the muscles of his carving arm, tensed, active.

Between them, a barrier,
        not material.
As if he lived within a mirror

working backward,
        putting images into the wood.
She looked for him there

after the work was done,
        the bench vacated,
the prints hung to dry . . .

was this evidence? Wood curls,
        tools,
a roller blackened with ink.

And once, a jolt more backward:
        the made things —
octopus, rooster, elephant,

and a face. Human. Her own face,
        the too-large nose, mouth, eyes
into one dimension distilled,

unmade from herself — swoop of inked line
        dark lip,
eyes without light,

speeding away from the source —
        but what source?
The wood? The blade?

EQUINOX

He is born at the community garden.
With a last hard push, his shoulders come out,
his forelegs fighting to lift out his haunches.
The impression of his hooves is driven into the soft soil.

~

In the church of my childhood, Christ on the cross was wood.
His skin had grain. The grain made me want to touch him.
I knew wood darkens with human touch:
if I touched him, the blonde pine would darken.
Darken to hickory. Darken to walnut.

~

He is shuddering with being born —
Does he feel he is always being born?
Weak and soil-stained, he is already as large
as an elk; he eats young grass,
pushes open the gate, trots down the sidewalk.
Beads of fluid drop from his penis,
at the center of each a nucleus, pollen-gold.
His antlers tear upward, branching,
the brown velvet rips from them.

~

And in that church, Christ had antlers —
no one there had forgotten that God courted the Madonna
as a palomino stag.
There was a painting of this gospel scene.
I stared at it forever.

~

Long ago, I saw him first as he was dying.
He stretched out his neck, the white patch visible
on his throat, uttered a hoarse cry as the fur fell away,
outgrown, He fell into the brown rot of the forest floor.
The flesh flies and black beetles settled upon him,

the vultures arrived, black wings hot under the sun.
They attended to their work — they carried him away.

ORIGIN

A spring night, already hot. He leaves his desk,
his work: military histories, pedigrees of Shepherd dogs.

Off the path, a baby sobs. Or is it a catbird?
No, it is a baby girl. He has always wanted a child.

Someone to remember him. He lifts her from
the ferns. Fortunate the bitch has just whelped her pups.

And the child lives on dog's milk. Petted by a gloved hand.
Calls him *uncle* when she learns to speak.

First she whimpers to her mother.
She growls before the human tongue is found.

The pups have blue eyes when born.
The blue eyes turn brown.

In the mirror, her muzzle is black and her ears sharp
triangles. Her blue eyes turn blue.

Moth Man

Maybe I am a woman in love,
or maybe I am delirious

in my attic room leaving the windows
open for the moth man —

A light on all night will draw him.

Inside the shade, he is small,
but when the sky turns soapy

he is longer than my body,
and fevered from the light bulb.

Crooked leg, plumes
of antennae, wing's false eye.

Is he drinking from the birdbath?
No, that is the wasp.

Does he want mulberry leaves and the violin recording?
No, that is the crickets.

Is he eating silver? Is he marching?
And the blue bug light —

Isn't it pretty?
I would die for that too,

accidentally dazzled.
Is he gold and white?
The pale green Luna?

Is he deep gray plush?
Will he ride my coat's woolen hem,

folded like a paper fan?
He is mine because I hide him.

ASKING

Tonight, the moon so white,
the black sky seems the material part —

The woman earlier, asking
Don't you ever get lonely?

As I thought the answers,
she asked about the scars under my hair.

I was hit by a car. When I was six.
I asked my mother if I was dreaming.

The moon tonight is so white —
I wonder how my mother answered.

In memory, I walk between rows of corn stubble,
gathering ears the harvester missed.

I wear my coyote ears. I was a coyote
that year. But that's not memory.

I always wore those ears.
I was always a coyote.

Mosquito

If she needed blood for her eggs —

If she asked … or did not ask, but

you understood by seeing —

the stem of her body, hollow,

and her face, half intent

and seeking, half inward-turned,

succumbing, and her body, after all,

not hollow, but swollen —

the ripe body of a brood mare,

her tail already wet with birthing fluid.

At the puncture itself, no pain:

a small, bearable itching.

You believe this time, seeing the black egg

momentarily clenched in the vulva,

then the black egg emerging,

whole and spherical, you can allow her

to continue — the blood drawn up

through the transparent proboscis,

the mare's forelegs bent, kneeling

upon your arm, the fluid rising

readily under the steady pressure.

The eggs pile up like bowling balls.

They resemble hematite —

the black surface reflects everything.

But you are not reflected.

You put your face against one

and do not see yourself. No, you must be

inside it — inside the egg, your knees

pulled up to your chin, your arms

holding your bent legs against your chest.

No Wonder

She looks across the table and sees.
Her lover is a plum.

How is it she's never noticed before?
No wonder his silence.

No wonder his good aroma,
like the heat of summer.

She has curled around him some nights
wondering at his growing softness —

He is so still, dark purple, black-purple,
curving into the dent

where his stem was.
Where he clung to the tree of his birth.

She lifts him from his place,
rubs him with her shirt tail.

His skin takes on an extra gloss.
It barely contains him.

Soon he will split, spilling
juice and veined, golden flesh.

She holds him up to her lips, her nose,
brushes his skin with her skin, pauses.

Reoccurring

The old slate floor with the cat's
eye in the corner. The cold flags
under your feet and the green
orb rolled into the corner and waiting.
A cold morning with the door
shut behind you — remember the silent
meowing of the cats behind the
pane? And the smeary windows
of the enclosed porch? Suddenly the idea
of an orange held aloft. The cat's eye
hadn't been there before. And then
it was. And then it was. You scooped it
up, cold glass against your cold fingers.
The orange held up. Just the idea
of the orange at that time. But later,
the cat's eye back in the house,
against a grey dish or found in a patch
of sun, when you picked it up, the orange
kept showing, like an image ghostly on a
Polaroid, but growing edges and depth.
Until that was the part that seemed real —
the orange and the heavy oriole landing,
making your arm bob. The oriole pecking
the flesh, keeping one eye fastened to you.

STANDING ON THE SEA WALL

— imagining my throat as a thin-walled teacup

holding a spoonful of gold
in solution. The presence of another —

a man

— largely in my dreams,
once woken from, no backward point of entry.

Goodbye, Goodbye,
my voice, protesting,

the voice, mute, *thinking* it.

To be changed to a green canary.

Shallow, I bargained.

My failure to change did not
leave me inconsolable.

Picture Book

Little wren, all anthro-
pomorphic, where is

the cork-like baby?
He lay down in a hollow

and was lost, though
you cried, you called —

maybe dried leaves
swept over him —

You put on your un-wren-like red
head scarf and "muffler" —

Why is he cork-like?
Because he is mute

and carvable and porous
and also organic, as in made

of living or once-
living material. Pray for floods

if you're serious. If you want
the hollows to yield him up.

GREEN ANOLE

Alone and lonely, I bought
a green anole.

I liked the way he clung to my finger
and pressed his fragile belly down
along its length.

"You need me, don't you?" I'd ask.
I held him to the window showing

him the snow piled up to either side of
silver paths of frozen boot prints.

"You'd never survive out there."
I set the thermostat to sixty
and carried him in my bra to keep him warm.

I felt humble, like a giantess
charged with the care of a tiny Indian prince.

I threw away my worn pastels
and bought sateens in gold and red.

"I'm going to put you
in your bower," I'd say.

Over the bra/anole, I layered
three or four shirts

and talked down the neck holes at him.
I ate pan-cooked kale for dinner that entire winter.

"I'd like a kale farmer to come get me out of this town.
I'd like a kale farmer to fuck me in his Georgia field of
        kale," I told the anole.

This was a diversionary lie.
In reality, I did not want to be touched.

At night I'd try to feel
my coccyx elongate

and grow down to the core
of the planet.

This was an exercise
to help me feel

as though I belonged
to the Earth.

"If that farmer has a wife
I'll fuck her too,"
I said to the anole.

He regarded me
with no visible alteration
of expression.

It was a pointless thing to say,
vulgar bravado,

and I could hardly muster any glee
 in my voice when I said it.

We lay in bed. I read
one book after another
and the white sky gradually darkened.

I ran a bath.
I hung the anole on the shower rod.
I think he appreciated the hot steam.

"Wow," I said, looking
at the anole, "wow."

The Secretary

The fox runs in the meadow and at the border of the meadow.

Up to the elbow and more, the fox occupies.

Someone tries to give you instruction, itemizing.

It sometimes seems like she's just briefly resting

over the arm, but you haven't seen it. Not lately.

He keeps talking, sometimes rapping the counter

with his knuckles. The fox which was an arm

rests on the desk, panting from her run.

You shouldn't stare at her, not while he's standing there.

Her legs marked with black socks, the thin line

of black between the red of her tail and the tail's white tip.

SPOOL STRETCHED

Spool is constantly resorted to to get lost or blind people from one place to another or from one place back again. Or does that amount to the same thing? Spool unraveling in a sweaty hand. Spool dizzy and losing substance. Spool stretched beyond her resources. Spool might be a line of colored pencil across a white, white page. Red pencil. The line runs off the page, across the table top, right up to the paring knife lodged in the wood.

Occasionally, Spool's thread runs out before the lost/blind person arrives at X. Empty Spool. Rue. Evergreens turning black as the sun descends. Crows coming together to roost at sundown. And Spool, in her mind's eye, sees the red line daintily skirt the upright knife, continue on.

First Beauty Lesson

My first time on my own. I lived in a mountain coal town.
I knew one person. I walked to see him every day,
even in winter, through the dump, up a tangled hill,

a house rough as a stable, a furnace, orange,
pulsing like a living carnelian,
where he moved inside the cast radius of light,

shadowed by light and sweat, the fire small in his pupils.
A pipe to give the glass its first shape,
tongs for growing it into shape.

I brought what I made: stories, folded paper animals.
What he made — thick bubbled goblets, green and gold bottles,
lacy sea horses — he never gave to me. He liked the rooms dark,

as if he were an elemental, like the salamanders
who live in flames. He worked until I stopped him,
when the windows darkened in the homes clustered in the valley.

He burnt what I brought. It fed the fire,
the fire made glass of it. He did not look
at what was finished. He made dragons, pegasi.

They flew — no, they were tethered.
They hung from the rafters by ribbon.
He was not affectionate, but he liked me there.

I washed him with olive oil soap. I slept on one side of his hay
stuffed bed. I drew or wrote. He made the solar system —
green Venus, silver Mercury. Mars was orange-red.

Like certain animals who stand as the hands pass over the
shoulder, sweep to the flank, he could be touched.
There was paper stuffed in the window frames' gaps;

snow made the world soundless. I looked for a long time —
his eyes, almost darkened, the fires low.
He lay under my palm. He did not stir or move or shy.

There was a red glass bird. And there was a real
one, later, flying from spruce to spruce.

DRAWING THE SELF-PORTRAIT

I request a set of watercolor pencils and a mirror.
The mirror delivered is small,
smaller than I'd wished for.

The reflection — a palomino unicorn.
You're pretty, I think, vainly tossing my head
to feel the white mane settle on the neck's arch.

The light is poor, but I can imagine the golden coat
under sun in an orchard clearing — airborne particles illuminated
and plums popping through their skins under my hooves —

so I draw the body highlighted, as it would be there.
I draw the dress so the small breasts shine up
out of the bodice as if each was lit by an interior bulb.

But oh — there is blood around the horn.
It's only blood. And the breasts —
the light is a kind of phosphorescent milk ...

The door is rattling. I look to it.
A man is there, his face obscured
by a green surgical mask, saying,

This one's been killing her foals.
I move the mirror down my torso, yes,
the low sexy mound of the abdomen —

gored. They are here to put down the mare.
Stupidly, I toss my head again,
the horn gouges the ceiling.

The mane falls like a hand stroking the neck.
I've not yet drawn the eyes.
The eyes are huge — liquid and empty of pupils.

OTTER AT A PARTY

"Going-away

party —

What's *that* supposed to mean?"

Steamer trunks

in the hall. The guest-
of-honor, also

the host, opens
the iron stove —

The fire makes the wood's innate energy visible
as fire.

One window persistently open — the hot
and the cool moving in — probably —

salamander-shaped eddies.

"It's a concept musical,"

Otter explains, not
for the first time.

"There's no production,
just a cast recording."

His listener nods the slow and long motion
of the 'dawning comprehension nod,'
though his eyes suddenly seem erased

with pencil and drawn back in neutral,
(but extra veiny,

        of course).

     He doesn't mean 'cast recording,'
     he means 'album.'

       "You used to be
       so much

       fun," no one even
       says. Not his wife,

diving now in the frigid backyard
fountain for lobbed sardines —

     a splash,

     drunken noises
     of approval follow.

A roll of school-style pull-down maps in the living room
and the host/guest-of-honor explains

his imagined route. On the far wall an age-damaged
mirror reflects some motion, some light.

You can only see it underwater —
the temporal silver bubbles caught

here and there
in her fur.

Silence, finger cymbals.

A ukulele
in the second act.

Lost Colony

Winter sky over the harbor —

white and purple as a frozen puddle,

black-rimmed, starred by its fractures —

makes me think *merciless.*

Alone, I am more alone in the winter light

(*but light does not start with mercy*).

The paper wasp at the birdbath — at the water's edge — the water's
circular shoreline and the red algae that grows on the cement.
The wasp drinks.

The bees at the beginning of autumn, circling the trash can. They crawl
into the caves of soda cans. They crawl out of the nectar caves
of soda cans.

The hornet caressing the flake of salmon on the breakfast plate —
his triangular head, the working jaws. He cuts himself a parcel of flesh,
soldiers it away.

Can I say it is a memory?
Leaving work the other night under the blue-white

mercury lights, I remembered: When I was born
the small spinning *everything* was gold. *We* were gold.

We slowed perceptibly. Some died.
Then many. Sky the color of today's sky —

mercury white,
the blue that dead bones should be.

Above us the gold turned.
Small things held us, preoccupied: pollen was gold,

the centers of flowers, black or gold, like us.
the gold changed, becoming white and distant.

How Does the Rhino Fly?

1

Some letters

sort of collapsing

on their stick legs.

2

Drawing wings on the sketch of the rhino.

3

Types of Impressions:

a spore print the mushroom cap
left on the white paper.

the absence of charcoal
in a gravestone
rubbing — letters and numbers
ghosting in a black field.

Not impressions.
A reflection?
The Shadow recalling
the Source.

4

The letters standing up

like foals, crooked and spindly.

Then frisking.

5

The rhino "taxi-ing," thick legs pumping, down the runway.
"What now?" when he takes off at the margin.

6

A new frame is what now.

Rehearsing your one-liners

in the great

acoustics

of the bathroom.

7

Back in the living room, a girl shadow puppet
gently taking the hand of an old, bent shadow puppet.
A goat shadow puppet observes, eating the scenery.

8

The letters B and
P passing on the street,

nodding
in recognition.

9

Now the rhino circles church ceilings
with the putti. You may see him one
Sunday if you glance up. He roosts
with the city pigeons over by the abandoned
movie theatre on Broadway. He's learned
how to drink on the fly like a bat. He preens
his pearl-grey wings with his horn.

ONLY SWEETNESS

Though I play the white noise
tape of the zebra finches
circling the aviary
often enough, I never dream
of flying, David.

I wonder how
they miked all 27
of those little birds —
catching each wing
beat and braiding

the beats into this sound
of heavy breathing over
a drum circle, but on finch
scale (think 4 oz. each). I did
once sort of hand feed this

oriole of some kind —
they like oranges and I
knew that. Have you ever held
a halved orange out
to a black and orange creature

waiting for him to understand
you mean no harm, you offer
only sweetness? And sometimes
you think *that's no oriole,
it's some kind of dog or even*

*a rail rider too weak to hop
a train out of here* and after
you are not too sure what

to believe, he hops or crawls
or drags himself to you, your

hand, the orange-half offering
and plunges his beak into
the fruit, gulping the flesh
into his own flesh, taking
greedy mouthfuls in a way

we associate with desperation,
but this oriole, this creature
is neither desperate or grateful.
So you wait, almost blank, gazing
at the lay of feathers against

his skull, the pips stuck to his beak.
You step up into the white noise.
He'll fly, you think, *if he finishes
the orange. Only half an orange
really.* But he never does, just stabs

or sips or laps and you keep holding
it out, your offering, feeling the percussive
strikes of the beak through the peel.
What could I do then, David,
once I saw so clearly there was nothing
else I wanted to do instead?

Night Work at Jeff's

Being, in a sense, a prop myself, I don't make suggestions to the photographer. But Jeff wants me to work overnight; he wants to watch the body grow more tired and weighty, wants the work to bend the body closer to the earth, as it is represented by the floorboards, the actual earth being three stories below. So I say I want to work with the bridle and his face shows his considering, his musing. "The bridle symbolizes restraint," he says.

I bring, as every time before, a lot of clothes, in my backpack and on hangers, but they remain unused. We get naked almost immediately, though he likes to work with the disrobing and robing as one of his subjects is Susanna and the Elders. We do some work with a washtub. First, I get in and out and hold a rag in my hand. Then we take turns lying next to it, with one body crouching over the other or in the tub, or the bodies in shifting, partially-tangled embraces, which we fumble hastily into having only eight seconds between frames.

Then we get the washtub and the rug it is on out of the way. I get the bridle down from the door and hold it. Jeff is preoccupied preparing. The bridle is very familiar. It means a lot to me. I hold it as tenderly as possible. If I could I would put the bit right in my mouth. Jeff moves about the space we shoot in, arranging lights and mirrors. Then he runs to one of the darkened, cluttered corners, fetching a prop. He brings back a dusty Calvary saddle, which he sets up on a sawhorse. The ladder is in the background. He's been working a lot with this ladder and a staircase as well that he'd built there inside the studio and which he drags into and out of the workspace. We have worked with the staircase together — he lays on it upside down and I clamber over him, climbing up and down the stairs in a crouch, on all fours — our limbs creating complicated knots or x-ings. The stairs and the ladder mean the connection of the heavens to the earth for him. I find it helpful to pretend I am a smart and curious animal while regarding his fallen body as I maneuver up and down over him, always mindful of the eight seconds between clicks.

At first we tug-o-war the bridle, our knees bent to lower our centers of gravity and our arms tense in resistance to the other's faked pull. Then I sling the bridle across my torso, the crown on my shoulder, the bit on my opposite hip. The reins I hold in one hand. Jeff helps me into the saddle. It is precarious on the sawhorse. We work out where I will look and what Jeff will do: climb the ladder, strain on tiptoe to whisper in my ear, reach up to me, cover my eyes, end on the ladder. We run through it and he changes the film again. And again runs into the depths of his possessions, bringing back a cheap headdress, the gaudy, necessary headband and feathers for a child's Indian costume. I put this on. We work with me on the saddle for a few more frames, then I get down.

The leather is not dusty where I sat. It glows where my thighs and ass rubbed and my ass is red and appealing-looking where the saddle exerted pressure. We both work at the ladder. He sits at the foot of it, trying to look dead and I climb the rungs. Then at his insistence I stand on his shoulders, squatting really, my crotch right at his eye level. I cling to the ladder, apologizing for causing him pain. He says he is fine. Then we both stand up. We've done a lot of work already. It is Friday night, not even midnight. I still wear the headdress. We move around the saddle a little. Jeff does the whisper thing. Is he an angel? Is this the Annunciation? Is he the Serpent? Am I Eve? Often I am, hand covering pubis, face aghast or benumbed. "I'm going to pick you up," he says. "This is the American photo, the groom on the threshold with his young and happy bride." We are nude except for my headdress. He stands to the side of the saddle. I am nervous I am too heavy. "This is our happiest day," he says. And we grin as the shutter closes over the lens.

SILENT DEFENSE

Rick, the beetle was dead.

Its legs were folded across its abdomen in a posture of containment

and decay was absent — its shell still coppery and lustrous.

Remember when I told you I'd been arrested for vandalism? —

I'd just wanted to taste one of the tiles on a particular cobalt pillar,

an unpremeditated act. I had a pocket knife with me by coincidence.

Rick, taste is important because speech is impossible.

The beetle's left elystron snapped off cleanly and fit the tip of my

tongue like the husk of a popcorn kernel. Still the throat did not

open. Maybe I was not surprised, though disappointed. I thought:

Well, a prose line is so useful when you can't stop talking,

but a significant part of my experience was *silence lapsed into*

as during an argument turning violent when at last there is no

recourse. I did not manage to bring the blue tile to my mouth;

a guard intervened. Rick, the beetle during its pupae stage is

seemingly inert though this is a stage of enormous physiological change.

The throat is like a well — imagine holding a beautiful object

in a closed well. What is the point — no light refracting through its

crystalline arrangement? It is a lump — black or grey or nothing.

Maybe you need to climb out. Carry it in your mouth, leave your

hands free for grasping.

MODEL

You agree to sit for
the miniaturist.

It takes all afternoon,
but you don't mind —

idly gazing out at
the crisp skeletons

of wildflowers poking
out of the snow.

Then he shows you
yourself, very small,

hands folded, eyes
far-off looking. *That's*

not me, you think
as he scoops you up

off the table top,
slides you into a glass tube,

stoppers it, and pockets
you and the little portrait

too, all clanking
in his coat, bumping his hip

all the way across
the field.

MEETING AME ON SUNDAY

His name is Ame.
And he is very big —

a circus attraction, he claims.
He exclaimed at my smallness.

But, Ame, isn't everyone small to you?
Ame, I asked if you were a Capricorn —

What a stupid waste of a question!
But you said we were opposites

and I thought of our birth times stuck apart
like two points on a Ferris wheel.

I've met guys like you before, Ame.
Guys I never see again. Shouldn't I have said

"Where can we meet again, Ame?
I bet I could love a big, fat guy

like you, a big body like you,
Ame." And not left before you agreed,

not turned waking in the box
of my room with its single window

into branches, into repeating triangles of roofs.
The circus gone.

Ame, I got your name.
That's a first.

WHITE CAT:

*A Narrative in Which the Hero Discovers
the Fulcrum of the Fairy Tale*

The Cup of Abundance is not what he had expected —
smaller than imagined, empty, though captivating, almost opaque, a
deeper-than-garnet red, and now he must merely lift it from its humble
pedestal in the otherwise empty tower room, and return to the family
— his human family who cast him out, hastily sentencing him to exile
after his conviction of the crime of destroying a fragile and prized
heirloom, which, the white cat being still a kitten (though in the late
stages) and thus a likely culprit, did *not* break. And the real culprit, his
foster brother, natural son to the dog who nursed him, to this moment
is still sheltered and cherished within their walls.

The white cat *has* mounted the tower stairs, *has* swum the Three Mile
River, *has* answered, correctly, the riddle put to him on the river's shore
by the old man, his lameness surely a deception, *has* guided the maiden
from the woods on a moonless night, saving her virtue and, possibly,
her life. He has befriended the young, ambitious, fortuneless man,
talented in mathematics and violin, and subsequently assisted the young
man in obtaining fortune, property, pretty wife, and influential father-
in-law. His ears repeatedly torn in fights with other toms in his first
weeks of homelessness are healed, but will never again be un-tattered.
His ribs are just visible. His flank and shoulder muscles rise as contours
under his coat.

It has been weeks or months since he ran across the garden at the sound
of his name or eaten meat scraps from his own crockery bowl. In fact,
at this moment, the string of sounds they used to signify him is lost,
as he regards the cup not much bigger, really, than an eggcup. And
the longing he felt, in those first weeks of exile, to hear his name, the
name they gave him, has dimmed or died to a twinge or less. It was

a lyrical name, something like 'Whiteness of Fresh Snow" or "Cow's Milk Moon." Something, he considers and allows, cumbersome on the tongue.

And no child's arms have encircled him and no clean towel folded into his sleeping basket. No sleeping basket whatsoever. Dry leaves scratched into a pile, mostly. But in regarding the Cup, the Cup allegedly, of Abundance, might they, after all, *not* accept his gift of penance, penance for *their* crime of mercilessness and capriciousness and lack of investigative rigor and not rub balm into his cracked paw pads and not lift down his bowl from the high shelf and fill it with diced chicken livers and not restore him to their guarded hearth, choosing instead to abide by their original, false judgment?

And in the absence, the utter denial of choosing to go without affection, has not his desire for the touch of a loving human hand almost been entirely conquered? And the itinerant's life with its killing of mice or rats in exchange for shelter in a barn or storeroom, the constant vigilance required by the dangers of the highway, and the frequent potential for subjugation to the vicious whims of other strays, cats and dogs alike, to say nothing of the wild things one encounters in ditches or brambles, seems, though lacking in any familiar tenderness, less risky, more foreseeable.

And this possible turn in his tale is clearly too, on the surface, most liberating and where the human hand will descend much less often, if ever, in love, so too will the restraining hand, the punishing one, be absent and never will the white cat succumb to a will not his own. The white cat's pupils dilate. The tower room is growing dark; the air swells with moisture in the twilight. The cup looks black. He can almost feel what it was to leave the cover of the hostas along the stone wall. To walk, then trot through the just-dewed grass toward the light-filled doorframe. It is his story. He has no name at all unless he wants it.

MECHANIZED

Everything is so sad

when one is longing for a machine
plumping the perfect dome

of steamed rice into a bowl on a conveyor belt under heat lamps.
Have you lost your love for the labor of human hands,
              the toiling heart?

There is a button with a peanut
icon, a button with a soybean icon.

Just whose baby's
got what kind of sauce?

Wait 'til it breaks —
you'll have to put your shame on the shelf —

running for the bright red (yes, of course)
emergency telephone,

Someone will be right there.

Wailing for the mechanic.
In a panic.

Whatever you make, in thanks, you'll make from scratch.

LETTER

Dear Dean,
Instead of a book, I could give you a sheet of these stamps

I made — which the United States Postal Service
does not recognize

as having any value,
monetary or otherwise.

I did one sheet for each
of the cats and if you look

closely you can see they only give the illusion of repetition —
the cats' expressions alter slightly in each.

Next I want to make a wooden goblet; would I
need a lathe? The last wooden cup I made is right now

drying on the dish rack.
Its bowl is about the size of half

a walnut. I can't give up drinking out of it
because I made it myself.

When I rise, thirsty, from my bed, in the dark, I go to the tap
with the cup. I fill it

and empty it, fill it, empty it. I keep my hand on
the faucet.

Fill, empty. About seventeen times
until I am satisfied.

Standing in the dark, I say "This simple cup is all I need"
and because I can hardly see

I get the impression I'm in the midst
of a radio interview. An interview

inside the radio. Then I make the mistake
of remembering Steve Martin

clutching all that stuff,
mournfully,

in *The Jerk*, especially the paddle
with the rubber ball attached by its elastic string.

I am holding a very small cup in my enormous hand.
I put it down gently, Dean, and I echolocate back to bed.

The Clearing

Oh!

You see it now — a pony
picking his way up the mountainside.

Even the needles on the evergreens,
        and the darker brown dapples on his brown coat

— at first his color seems solid, but it isn't so —
        And you think — or no,

you know what you see.
        Those years ago, the sad lover forcing your chin,

        he didn't know he wasn't being gentle,
he'd hold the chin (he wanted the eyes to look at his)

What are you looking at?

You never could say.

You looked into empty corners of the bedroom and saw nothing.

Or you could not say what you saw.

You could not speak.

You looked.

You looked up.

And now. To see it clearly — the dark back,
the shoulder bones shifting under the hide, the careful working

of his legs. To see even the darker spots
upon the brown coat. They spread from withers to rump.

And see the needles, individual, on the evergreens,
and marks on the rocks, marks that show where they cleaved,

where water, freezing, broke the mountain upward.

INTRUDING MEMORY

The window at the landing

where the stair turns — each pane

arranging its portion —

my foot descending,

the pointed toe plunging toward the tread,

the bare foot, the infant toes above

a moving landscape — I think I was harnessed

beneath the carriage of a huge balloon,

reeled out to nap as one reels out laundry

to dry from an upper-story window.

My mother busy tidying above,

tossing the scraps of a meal overboard.

And just before sleep, my new eyes

noting the backs of birds diving

after the meal's detritus — apple peelings,

uneaten bread crust — below that,

a mile or more, green pastures,

a tractor dragging harrows,

combing the earth …

CRASH LAND

— For RTH

Like a sad clown left out
in serious weather —

possibly also angry.
I was born with the sun, he says.

Any sort of obvious
disguise works best —

if there are holes
artificial becomes *artful.*

Is hydrogen desperate
to become

helium? Always
projecting

my Internal on
another's External —

like personifying atoms
or preoccupations with Hyena

eviscerating her prey —
simultaneously and brokenly

trying not to damage
the other's External.

I'm not from
here, he keeps

trying to tell
me / succeeds in telling me.

Ignoring the leg bone
with a thin bit of hide still attached

I drag perpetually about
in my jaws? Or

is it not visible?
When an alien crash-lands

on the veldt does Hyena
hear it, looking up

from a mouthful
of viscera?

What is this
substance you

are made of? I wonder
on behalf of

myself & on behalf
of this Other.

It was getting really complex
just trying to concept-

ualize my own
pieces; so what

can one deduct about
another? A burnt smell

from entering this
atmosphere and the calcium

obviously some key
compositional element

and the hunger
some combination of one

and one. There is salt
on his External,

an essential mineral
I savor.

My disguise
is full of holes.

That is how
it hides me.

CROSS POLLINATION

What pollinates the cross-
stones? No *emerald*, no *ruby-*

throated. Something blunt,
something blind. Roll them

like dice, they come up Xs.
The Xs of dead eyes.

Franz Wright says crosses
are short-hand for bodies.

Bodies playing airplane.

These aren't that kind
of cross.
Being equilateral.

Wind pollinates the poppies
and then sometime later
pollinates the corn. Cross-

stones, not wind-touched,
might be pollinated by a chill

dribble of water
lofting little golden grains

from croci stamen all
dreaming of being

saffron. A gentle hand
wielding a paint brush

introduces Prof. Plum to
Ms. Apricot. The resultant

offspring grows up,
goes into law enforcement:

meet Inspector Plucot.

UNIFORM

He loved his uniform.
                    — Dean Young on Apollonaire

His uniform was purple with ostrich feathers.

It was a burlap sack, mechanic's coverall,

a hair shirt, a bandleader's red jacket,

his barbecue apron, *Kiss the Cook*,

his rag-soft flannel,

his T-shirt: *MoMA, Coors, Carpe Diem*.

It had brass buttons, zigzag stitch, braided cord,

passport pocket, zippers, stays, vent cut.

It was his last suit

and his first.

His skin was pale under clothes

and golden where sun touched

the hair of his upper lip,

the hair on the back of his hands.

At last, his uniform was the body:

a coat over bones,

an overcoat,

the sheet laid down over wreckage.

But it was not wreckage,

vacated, it had no sorrow, no grief.

He wore it out,

out of doors.

At last it tore at the seams,

fell into rags.

He was naked without it,

naked he went —

About the Author

Rosalynde Vas Dias was born and raised in Eastern Pennsylvania. She received a B.A. in English in 1999 from DeSales University, a small liberal arts college in the Lehigh Valley region of Pennsylvania and holds an M.F.A. in Poetry from Warren Wilson College. She has lived in Providence, Rhode Island since 2002, where she has supported herself by working as an administrative assistant, temp worker, occasional life model, and private poetry teacher. She currently is the bookkeeper for a large-scale live music venue in Providence.